Why E

An Introduction to Real Estate for
Aspiring Entrepreneurs

Why Real Estate?

An Introduction to Real Estate for Aspiring Entrepreneurs

Jeffrey Stump

YouSpeakIt
PUBLISHING
The Easy Way to Get Your Book Done Right™

www.YouSpeakItPublishing.com

To Jose, for getting me into my favorite game and never letting me play it at less than my best.

Contents

Acknowledgments

STOP!

If you read books the way I do, you're thinking about skipping the acknowledgments.

This isn't just any book though; it's a book for people interested in starting to invest in real estate, and if you're one of them, there's an important lesson in this section:

I did not do it alone.

Not even close. Chances are you won't either. So, skim over my list, and then take some time to reflect on the people who do or would support you. Make your own list of the people you know who already want you to succeed. When you're done with this book, it'll be time to start calling them!

I'd like to express my gratitude to:

Lane, for challenging me to think bigger and for all the guidance he's given me about Portland real estate.

Livier and Jose Sr., for welcoming me into their family, for being unbelievably good housemates, and for all the delicious Mexican food.

My father, because now I realize that I'm doing the same thing he tried for so long to teach me.

My mother, for all the fortitude it took to watch her odd-ball son go from unemployed to hundreds of thousands of dollars in debt—and still unemployed—while loving him just as much the whole time.

Ben, for keeping me accountable for my finances, my writing, and my stomach fat.

Sarah, for all the fights with customer service agents she's had on my behalf.

Linwood, for believing in me even before I did.

Majid, for trusting me to do what I say and giving me the opportunity to live up to it.

Beth, for making me take breaks on weekends.

Deanne, for reminding me of the progress I'm making, even when it seems so slow.

My grandfather, for giving me a once in a lifetime opportunity and a bigger head start than anyone deserves.

Nikki, Linda, Ashley, Aaron, Jill, Tatiana, Dani, Jeffrey, Danny, Brad, Sid, Shawn, Lisa, Nick, Tonya, Kim, Ron, and all the other real estate professionals who've helped me learn.

Maura, Keith, Cameron, Nida, and all the other team members with YouSpeakIt Book Publishing who made this book possible.

Introduction

This book explores some of the basic principles that drive real estate and make it a lucrative proposition for people who decide to invest their time in this fascinating field. If you are curious about real estate and trying to determine if it is something you want to investigate more, this is a book for you.

From my years of experience in real estate, I have come to realize that some real estate concepts are not very well understood by the general public.

For instance:

- Did you know that debt can actually create wealth through inflation?

- Did you know that the government specifically encourages real estate development?

- Did you know that the federal government subsidizes many people who purchase homes for the first time?

I have also come to realize that some of the most basic and lucrative real estate concepts are often not understood even by otherwise sophisticated homeowners. Most people aren't familiar with these kinds of facts, and it seems to me that they might make different decisions if they were more knowledgeable—and they might be well- rewarded.

I've written this book because, in short, I think we need more real estate investors. I see real estate investors as people who think economically about the spaces in which we live and the value they provide and then think about how they could be better. In doing so, they can help to make the world a better place.

A real estate investor is responsible for forming the built environment and bringing that built environment back to the public, who wants and needs to use it. We bring it back better than it was before in whatever way we identify that people will value. Our environment can be changed for the better in many ways. The possibilities are literally endless, so let's get started!

You may already have some ideas. My particular passion is *new urbanism,* which is the idea that neighborhoods can be made more attractive and more environmentally friendly by walkability and a wide range of housing and job types. I work on that by pursuing urban infill development in the Portland, Oregon area. Most of our projects are apartment complexes that add value by providing more opportunity for people to live in or close to this desirable city.

The new residents benefit from the quality of life that Portland can provide, and the city itself benefits from having more community members who pay taxes, shop, put together Meetup groups, go dancing, and participate in all the other happenings that citizens in a city enjoy. All those activities create value, and that value reaches more people when they can be done closer together.

Cities help people—in more ways than I can discuss here—but they also need people to help them grow and thrive. Most cities will create a zoning code that generally outlines what they want to happen inside them, but they lack the knowledge, skills, and resources to actually create any of it.

If you are an aspiring entrepreneur, this is where you come in.

You may be under the impression that, as a small investor, you're at a disadvantage. However, you can see and do things that the big guys can't. For example, through your own observations, you may be able to tell that a house will rent better because it's next to a major transit line. You can buy it for less because you don't have to pay an acquisitions officer a hundred dollars per hour just to look at it.

This book is not intended to be a how-to book on real estate investing. There are many other resources better suited for that purpose. *Bigger Pockets Inc.*, found at biggerpockets.com, is one of them; it's a free forum that can provide you with valuable information. I would recommend it for anyone exploring the tactics of real estate investing.

Nothing in this book is meant to be financial advice—I want to make that clear. You'll have to look at your own situation to decide what's right for you.

If you are relatively new to the world of real estate investing, this book was written especially for you. It is meant to inform you about the opportunities that real estate provides and to help you gain a new understanding of some important facets of the business.

After reading this book, I hope you see that investing in real estate can be fun and exciting, as well as lucrative. It can be a satisfying and profitable way to make the world a better place.

CHAPTER ONE

The Control Premium

MAKING SOMETHING BETTER

After reading the title of this chapter, you may be asking: *What is a control premium?*

Simply put, the control premium refers to whatever it's worth to be the one making the decisions.

What is it worth to you to be the one in the driver's seat?

Suppose a company is run by majority vote of its shareholders. Imagine you own 50 percent of the shares, and a stranger owns the other 50 percent.

How much more than the usual price would you pay for the one additional share that would let you control the company?

The answer to that question is the control premium, and it depends more on who you are than what the company is worth. If you're not interested in the company, if you don't understand what it does or why, you should probably pay nothing. If, however, you're an expert in the industry, intimately familiar with the operations, and have insight into the problems the company is dealing with, you may be willing to pay a great deal to control the direction of the company. In your hands, the company may be a much more valuable tool for creating value than in someone else's hands.

Think of it this way: A master carpenter could do more with a hammer than the average person could. Their experience and knowledge allow them to make better use of the same resources.

If you care about your mission and actively seek the knowledge and skills for its progress, you will soon be the most qualified person to lead the mission—if you aren't already. The more you invest in your own skills, knowledge, and network, the more value you'll be able to create. When you control an enterprise for which you've prepared yourself, you are much more likely to increase the value of that enterprise.

Keep in mind: No one else knows how much you know. When you walk up to a person who owns a piece of real estate, you may have an ocean of knowledge behind you or just a puddle. They can't tell. If you have a genius idea that can double or triple the value of a piece of real estate, that idea is yours and yours alone until you're generous enough to share it with someone.

Someone selling you property will generally have no idea what your control premium is; nor should they. It's not their business. If you buy their house, then double its value, good for you. They don't deserve any credit for your plan and your work.

Don't get caught up with worrying about whether you pay the control premium or keep it to yourself. Just be sure you know what the control premium is because it is closely related to the core value proposition of the entire business of real estate.

What is that core value proposition?

Are you ready?

Write this down:

THE CORE VALUE OF REAL ESTATE IS TO CONTROL VALUABLE ASSETS.

It really is that simple.

The idea of controlling valuable assets has two major parts:

1. The selection of assets
2. The value of assets

The first part, you understand already. You select assets based on your knowledge, skills, and connections. The assets you should choose are the ones that you believe you can manage better than other people can. The second part is just math; the more valuable the asset you control, the more value you create with your skill.

If you're going to double the value of a thing, don't you want it to be as valuable as possible?

Wouldn't you rather double the value of a skyscraper than a mousetrap?

We'll cover more about this later. Note that I haven't said anything about money. This was no accident. *It's about control, not about capital.* If you have money, great—go ahead and use it—but remember it's all about control, not money.

It is typical for an entrepreneur to control a project with a minimum of their own capital; just a few hundred dollars—or maybe nothing at all—may control an asset worth hundreds of thousands. The extent to which the entrepreneur's direction leads the project to excess value is the extent to which the entrepreneur is rewarded.

Become the person who takes a position of control and earns rewards—or consequences—accordingly. Put yourself in the driver's seat of your work and earn by your own courage and vision. Take full ownership of your decisions, good and bad. Your rewards will go far beyond the scope of what I can describe in this book; they are easily the greatest value real estate offers.

Identifying Opportunities

You already possess the ability to look at the world around you and use your observations to identify ways that the world can be better. I hope this isn't news to you. It applies to everything around you, including real estate. Because you live in a particular place, you have knowledge specific to that place, and that knowledge can help you. What this means is that, right off the bat, because you have a thinking brain and some location-specific knowledge, you can create value. You already have some natural ability. The more thinking you can do and the more knowledge you have, the more value you can create, but you can also use what you already know to start searching for opportunities.

Fantastic opportunities will keep passing you by if you fail to recognize them. However, if you can learn to see even just a few different types of opportunities, you will be amazed at how quickly you will find yourself overwhelmed by the large number of options that appear. You will then need to learn how to pick only the best ones.

You'll need to study what the real estate industry is doing in your particular neck of the woods before you really focus on any one strategy. I recommend learning a few different strategies to create value. When you have accumulated some knowledge, go looking for places where those strategies could be put to good use.

There are many strategies to choose from, and here are a few suggestions:

- If you live in an area that is growing, but where not many people currently live, consider a *buy, fix, and rent* strategy. Using this tactic, you pay for some new real estate with bank money, pay for the bank money with rent money, and you keep all the difference.

- If you live near many wealthy single-family homeowners, consider a strategy in which you buy houses that need work, repair them, and sell them for a profit.

- You could specialize in finding rundown houses that are set among nice homes. Improving these houses can bring their value up substantially.

- If you live in an urban area that is growing rapidly, consider buying apartment buildings that need some repairs; you can improve them and resell them.

Whatever it is you decide to do, get good at it, and learn how to identify the best opportunities.

Once you are comfortable with and intimately understand a strategy, you'll want to plan it out.

Creating Your Plan

Have you already identified an opportunity to improve a real estate scenario?

If you've identified an opportunity for a better *anything,* give it serious consideration. Because you're close to it, because you believe in it, because you've personally figured out what it is, chances are that you are the best person to take it to the next step. You are going to understand better than anyone else what it is and how it can be done.

That understanding is what will help you create a plan for making the improvement that you've identified. Put your plan on paper or a spreadsheet and be sure that it's crystal clear. It is the most valuable thing you'll create, and it is the best place to put your efforts at this point. Make your plan detailed enough so that it could be accomplished by anyone else.

Truth be told, once you've planned how to take advantage of the opportunity effectively, if that plan is convincing, you need not even do it. You can sell it to someone else, or you can pay someone else to do it for you, and you can move on to finding another opportunity and creating another plan.

Remember, to make any of this possible, you must:

- Know what you want to do.
- Think it through in a clear and concise way.
- Document it so others can follow your plan.

Executing Your Plan

So, let's imagine you have found an opportunity to create value, and you have a plan to make good on it. Great! You've observed the world around you, you've seen an opportunity, and you've planned how to take advantage of it. These are the most valuable things you can contribute.

You've already done the hard part, and now you have some options. It's up to you where you want to go from here.

Do you want to sell your idea?

At this point, if you think your idea has merit, but you can't put it into motion—or you just don't want to—you can sell your idea. You just need to find someone who wants to execute it. In the industry, we call this *wholesaling*.

Do you want to see your plan through yourself?

If you are excited about your idea and want to forge ahead, that's wonderful. Real estate offers that opportunity. Whenever we buy a piece of real estate, we are buying the power to execute our plan. When we buy a piece of real estate, we are also buying the legal authority to take whatever our idea is to make the world better and implement it ourselves, within the bounds of whatever our city allows, of course.

This is what I like most about real estate: It gives us an ability to claim the credit for all our personal power, for all our knowledge, and the opportunities we see. When we act to improve the world around us, we can see the results of our actions come back to us, to our clients, and to other people who benefit from our improvements.

Money Wants a Deal

Do you have an idea that you're excited about but are hesitating to move forward?

In my experience, the most common roadblock here is that many people don't know where the money will come from to execute their plan. Don't worry; money wants a deal. Money *craves* a deal.

If you understand the opportunity, have found a good place to apply it, and have planned for it appropriately, you soon won't have to worry about money.

You have one last skill to cultivate, and that is the ability to communicate your confidence in your plan. You need to be able to take all the knowledge and work you've already put into the deal and convey to other people how good it is. Let them know you are generous enough to give them the opportunity to invest with you, and soon you'll have people asking you to borrow their money.

CONSOLIDATING THE POWER YOU NEED

A lot of people are kept out of real estate because of their inability to follow through.

You might have an idea, but you haven't taken the time to sit down and think about it. Or, you might think about it, but haven't hashed out the details and written out a plan. Or, you might write a plan, but stop there because you fear you won't be able to follow through. You might be afraid your idea isn't good enough. You might be afraid you can't afford to proceed.

Whatever the reason, this inability to follow through prevents many people from acting even though they know they could do some good for themselves or for others.

How do you find the power to move forward?

This section is about accumulating, in a very broad sense, the power to make happen the things we want to happen. The details are numerous, but we can divide the elements of this power into three different foundational categories.

These categories are:

1. Your personal power
2. Your network
3. Your finances

Each of these foundational elements, which we will discuss below, is a necessary part of producing change in the world.

Your Personal Power

Personal power includes your unique skills, knowledge, and abilities. This includes all the things you can do well using your own hands, feet, and head. Your personal power is the most important of the three foundations of power.

How can you consolidate your personal power to make yourself more capable of executing the ideas that you have?

Work on your skills. Study and educate yourself. Your knowledge is what allows you to make better decisions. The more you increase your abilities, the more confidence you will have—and others will have—in yourself to make more important and better decisions.

Think about all the industries that have been built around making good decisions. Engineers, teachers, doctors, lawyers, and accountants all earn their money by helping people make better decisions.

Do you think it might help you to know some of what they know?

Absolutely it would! Even if you hire people to help you, they'll never understand your situation better than you do. Understanding the issues will always give you a leg up in making sure your problems are solved the best way.

Remember, the investments you make in yourself can never be taken away.

Physical and mental improvement and maintenance are also in the realm of personal power. I find that not only does regular exercise and relaxation help me feel better; it also improves my work. Good health needs no other reason than itself to be worthy of pursuit, but many of the things I do to maintain and improve my personal health have dramatically improved my ability to perform in my business as well.

Caring for my body throughout each day helps me maintain my energy during work and play at a higher level and for longer. In this way, clean eating, exercise, and meditation not only bring me the joy of a healthy body but raise my productivity and income as well.

Study the skills that are important to you, and study some peripheral skills as well, so you can interface with those aspects of the community better. The better developed your physical and mental abilities, the more you will be able to support the execution of your ideas.

Your Network

Your network can simply be defined as the people you know, but I would clarify the definition further in this way: Don't throw out any connection because you think they don't know, like, or trust you well enough. You need all the connections you can get, and once they smile when you call, they're your friend.

As I've stated, building personal power is by far the most important foundation of power, but building a good network is what will set you apart from everybody else.

During your day, you only have so many hours to do the things you want to do, and you will only be able to study so many topics and learn so many things. Eventually, you run into some limitations, whether they are due to lack of time, knowledge, money, or contacts. There is a huge range of factors that can limit us, not because we are underperforming, but simply because we're human.

That is why we need to have teams work with us.

Contacting and developing relationships with people who can help you accomplish what you want is the second foundation of power. This is my personal favorite means to power. I surround myself with skilled and capable people of all different types who believe in me and want me to succeed. When I need help, or I run into an obstacle that I cannot or do not want to overcome myself, I go to one or more of them to ask for help.

When I started on my journey into real estate, I was fortunate to have friends and family who loved me; and truthfully, they have more claim to anything my company has done than I do myself. If you know people who can—and would—help you, take note and talk with them. If you don't know any, don't worry, most people are just waiting for you to show that you recognize that friendship is a two-way street. Go be a friend, and you'll soon have a friend.

Your Finances

The last foundation of power is the most touted: money itself. Since so many people feel limited by this foundation of power, I'd like to say a bit about what money is and what it is not. What it is most certainly *not* is limited; money, after all, is *imaginary*. More money can be created. It is created every time a bank makes a loan.

Did you think only the Federal Reserve could create money?

Think again; if a bank can lend out the money that you deposit there to another person, who then takes that money and deposits it in another bank, what do you think that bank will do with it?

The bank will lend it out again. Then, that borrower will deposit it somewhere and the cycle will keep going around until there is as much money as the banks have the courage to lend. For this reason, skilled businesspeople can raise essentially unlimited quantities of it. You will also be able to do this when you understand how.

So, how do we define money?

Money is very like *shared confidence*. When you offer it, it inspires others to act, and the offer lets them know that you are sure about what you want. If you had the money for it, you could pay some employees to come along with you on an adventure they had no understanding of and no expectations for. You could pay some contractors to do a job they didn't understand the purpose of and didn't know who actually wanted the job done. Paying someone won't help you if the thing you're doing is wrong, foolish, or frivolous, but the people you're paying will probably continue to help you—at least, until you run out of money.

People who consider buying real estate for the first time always seem to worry about how they'll afford the down-payment. The entrepreneur's answer is to borrow the money. But, having some money of your own can make it easier and faster to execute your projects when it allows you to pay your down payment yourself instead of having to find someone else who is willing to pay it for you.

My favorite thing to do with money, however, is to buy myself time. Time, unlike money, is not imaginary, is not replaceable, and will always be a limiting variable, so I look for ways to purchase more of my own time back.

Are you doing something that takes up your time and doesn't bring joy to your life, but is important and worthwhile?

If you can find someone who does like to do that thing, then pay them to do it. They'll be happy to ply their trade, and you'll be happy to be out of their trade.

Do not neglect any of these three foundations. As you build each one up, you'll find that you're gradually able to take on more and more ambitious projects, which will be more satisfying to you and will add more value to yourself and your network.

PROTECTING YOURSELF

It's great to have an idea, and it's great to pursue it, but while you're doing that, you can't lose touch with reality. Reality can sometimes be a little harsher than we'd like to admit. This section is about setting expectations realistically. It is about planning wisely to secure the best possible outcome and making sure that you are reasonably protected against the worst possible outcomes.

Hedging Against the Weak Points in Your Plan

Plans are wonderful and necessary, but things rarely ever go exactly according to plan. Making a good plan requires a large degree of honesty with yourself.

- Is your plan realistic?
- Is it based on reasonable expectations?
- Can you explain it clearly to someone else?

To help protect you from failure, you must have the wisdom to recognize where the plan may come apart or when you may not yet be ready to execute part of the plan. Once you balance the expectations, weak points, and the goals of your plan, you can decide whether the plan will really be a good one to pursue.

Sharing Your Responsibilities With Your Team

One of the most common weak points in a plan, particularly an ambitious one, is that it may incorporate activities for which you're totally unqualified.

That's a good thing. It means you're challenging yourself.

However, you certainly don't want to depend on yourself to do things you aren't qualified to do. The good news is that real estate is a massive and mature industry. Even if you were qualified to do all the different tasks in a project, no one would expect you to, and you probably wouldn't want to either. There is an enormous number of different professional specializations, with different licenses required, and contractors that you can depend on to get those jobs done.

Assemble a team to do those activities which you are either unqualified to do or are uninterested in doing. Have the honesty to admit to yourself whenever either of those two is the case. Leaning on your network will take you a long way toward accomplishing more of your real estate goals.

Limiting Your Downside

Let's say you have a good plan. You know what the weak points are. You're confident in its purpose, and you have assembled the best team to execute it.

What do you do if it goes wrong anyway?

First, you should have insurance for your title to the land, for your building, and for lawsuits that may come against you for accidents that occur on your property. Title disputes, earthquakes, fires, injuries, and the like occur from time to time. You should shop around, but an efficient insurance company should be able to insure you against major losses. Make sure you insure any borrowers who help you purchase or pay for things on the property.

Second, since you know what the weak points in your plan are, make sure you do something about what you'll do if the plan falls apart at one of those weak points.

Is there a strong chance the plan will take much longer than it should?

Then, get a guaranteed maximum price from your contractor, so they know you'll require them to stick to their numbers. The reason we write contracts is so that we know ahead of time what needs to be done if things don't go the way we meant them to. So, include as many of these contingencies as you can foresee in your documents.

Third, if you're really doing real estate the way it's most powerful, you'll be borrowing other people's money. In this case, you need a plan to return their money to them even if your plan doesn't work out at all. The most common way this is done is to buy properties only at a discount. That means buying from people for whom the simple act of the sale is a service to them, so you can buy the property for less than it's normally worth.

For example: if you borrow $270,00 to buy a property that is normally worth $300,000, then your plan doesn't work out, you should still be able to sell the property again with enough proceeds to pay back the $270,000 that you borrowed.

Fourth, and not the last, but the last that we'll cover here, is partners. Sometimes, there simply is no practical way to honestly promise someone that you will be able to pay them back. In this case, whoever is giving you money to make your plan work must know that they are sharing with you the risk of your plan failing.

If you borrow money and are unable to protect your ability to pay it back, whoever you borrowed it from needs to know that. And, if it means they don't let you use the money, then so be it. You'll need to find someone who isn't afraid to take that risk.

CHAPTER TWO

The Owner-Occupied Advantage

A ROCK-STAR TENANT

If you want to get started in real estate and you currently have a full-time job, but don't have much cash or real estate experience, the obvious place to start investing is in the place where *you* live. There are some advantages associated with a property that is your residence, especially here in the United States. The U.S. Government is extraordinarily friendly to homeowners and wants people to buy and live in their own houses. I've been surprised by the number of people who don't realize the competitive edge that they can have here.

Before we proceed, I'd like to make a note about perspective. There are two kinds of home ownership: economic and consumer. Consumer home ownership is about having what you want and enjoying it because you choose to be good to yourself. A sixteen-million-dollar home in Beverly Hills is a consumer home. This chapter is about *economic home ownership,* the kind that helps you make money. Therefore, in this chapter, I'd like you to think of yourself *as a renter* in the home you are in or are considering buying for yourself.

Do your planning and calculations as if someone else were going to live in the home and pay you for the privilege. If the property doesn't make sense from that perspective, even though some of the information in this chapter might help you squeeze more out of it, you're probably better off doing something else.

When you find a property that could make enough in rent to cover all its expenses with a little left over, take some time to learn about first-time homebuyer benefits. The information in this chapter will help you on your way.

An owner-occupant has many advantages that are not enjoyed by an owner who leases their property to someone else. Getting a deal that is good enough to rent while being run as a business is difficult. Doing this for the first time is even more so, keep these advantages in mind to help build your courage to move forward.

To start, these three benefits are yours from the outset:

- On-time rent payments
- Good care of the premises
- No need for contracts and tenant communication

On-Time Payments

The first advantage you have when you're buying for yourself is you can be sure about the performance of the tenant. Other landlords will have to plan for messy, delinquent, and litigious tenants, but not you. You will pay your mortgage on time, as well as your insurance and utilities. Being certain of good tenant performance is one of the biggest advantages to occupying a home you own—and it has financial value. Landlords who are renting out single-family homes are advised to budget 5 percent of the gross rent to handle tenant delinquency and vacancy. You should too, but in this case, you know there is no risk.

Taking Care of the Premises

Besides treating the property with respect, you'll also be more reliable with your property care than anyone else would be.

You know you're not going to hoard junk in the living room. You know that you will replace the batteries in the smoke detectors when you need to because you care about your safety and the integrity of the building that you bought.

You will keep to a budget. You will pay your homeowner's insurance on time because you can set it up to auto-deduct. You can pay your utilities and your mortgage payments on time by setting them up to auto-deduct as well.

You don't have to go as far as paying yourself a check every month, but make sure that you have budgeted for all the expenses of the household. When you understand the expenses of renting your home as if it were on the market, this will allow you to be much more consistent than a typical tenant would be, and this will make your investment safer and more tax-efficient as well.

Contracts and Communication

If you are the tenant, you can easily skip through the whole contracting process that you would typically provide for a tenant, and this is a great advantage. When you are a landlord, you must contract with and communicate clearly with renters. In addition, you might also have to contract with other parties to help manage the rental and the physical property.

For any rental, you'd be required to create a lease agreement, including a long list of notices detailing all the things you require the tenant to do as part of the agreement, including what is not allowed, what they would have to pay fines for, and when they need to notify you. When you are the tenant, all this paperwork is rendered unnecessary, saving you time and money.

In total, these three issues—the care of the premises, the on-time payments, and the ability to skip through all the contracting and legalese—can increase the monetary value of the property. You are the perfect tenant. With you as a renter, the property would require much less work than renting to a stranger and would naturally be more profitable. It may seem kind of strange to think of yourself as your own tenant, and these advantages may seem trivial, but they are not. Most of the industry operates profitably with these as their primary struggles. When you do the same deal, every dollar you save goes straight to profit and can make a deal safer for you.

AN AWESOME MANAGER

Under normal conditions, I would never recommend that you manage a property yourself. Professional management is expensive, but it is worth the money. However, in the case of your own home, when you are your own tenant, it certainly makes sense for cost-efficiency. You're managing yourself!

Believe it or not, this gives you a big advantage over most deals, which require substantial and professional management. As I've said, professional management is worth it, but since you won't need it for a property you live in, you have another financial edge. Taking care of your own property increases the cost-effectiveness, efficiency, and peace of mind of your real estate enterprise.

Highly Cost-Effective

Why am I so sure that professional management is usually best?

When I started with my first rental, I attempted to manage it myself, and it was a disaster. I had lots of better things to do than study landlord-tenant law. Since I didn't study, I didn't understand all the things that were necessary to do to make sure I was properly servicing my tenants. As a result, they received lower-quality service from me than they should have. I also wasn't protecting myself. I wasn't making sure that I was doing all the things that a landlord needed to do in order to be recognized by the law as legitimate, in case a problem should arise.

Management activities are time-consuming. In the process of managing the property myself, I also had to give up many other activities I could have been doing. Ultimately, I saved very little money by hustling away at a task for which I was not qualified. I recommend you not do the same.

With every other project you ever do, hire a property manager, but in the case of an owner-occupied building, you are your own tenant. You don't need to have a manager; you won't worry about suing yourself. The savings in time, money, and energy are a real advantage.

Highly Efficient

When I finally realized I was not up to the task of management, I hired a management company to replace me. That turned out to be my next mistake.

They were excellent marketers. They answered the phone immediately, responded very quickly to my requests, and in general, did a very good job of making me feel well cared for.

However, problems soon arose. When I checked on their listings on behalf of our property and inspected the property to see what needed to be done and what had been done, I found that they weren't doing much of the work they had been hired to do. I had been sold a promotional concept of how great this management company was, and then I was essentially getting no service. They were taking a cut of the income from the property and doing nothing.

Overseeing a management company is another task you commonly take on when you rent out a property. You save yourself this hassle and expense when you are your own tenant.

In summary, when you're renting to yourself, there is a whole slew of people problems, bidding problems, contracting problems, and legal problems that you won't have to deal with at all. When you're renting to yourself, there is no need to hire and pay anyone else for legal contracts or property management. You won't have to worry about how your manager is performing. You'll spend less time and effort planning and coordinating between different parties that could potentially influence your property. These factors will help you financially and allow you to maintain more peace of mind.

SPECIAL TREATMENT

Besides the basic benefits we have just mentioned, homeowners are treated differently from landlords in several legal and financial ways that will be helpful to you. They give an owner-occupant an edge over other investors in the real estate game.

For an owner-occupant investing in a single-family home, here are a few examples:

- Single-family homeowners often get better deals on mortgages.

- There are unique opportunities that can help ease purchase of a single-family home.

- Buyers and sellers of single-family homes are abundant in the real estate world.

- There may be significant tax advantages, which we will discuss in the next chapter.

If you haven't yet purchased your first property, or if you are having trouble seeing the advantage of it from a business standpoint, then hopefully this section will clear up that issue for you.

Mortgages

I have a friend who helps me buy houses in Portland, Oregon, but I'm afraid that I won't be able to get his help anymore because he only ever wants to pay for about 50 percent of the house. If I need to come up with 50 percent of the value of a $400,000 house, that's still $200,000! You might be able to see how that could be a problem.

In any situation, the same two issues tend to limit what I can do: time and money. If, like me, you are at least occasionally limited by money, then you will need capital partners who will pay a lot more than 50 percent loan-to-value.

Homeowners are treated differently than other investors in mortgage matters. There are federal agencies that insure homeowner mortgages and allow them to be created at a much higher loan-to-value ratio—which means less of your money and more of theirs—and at lower interest rates. Those are both good things for you. The higher loan amount increases the efficiency of the project dramatically, and the reduction of the interest rate increases the profitability.

A Thick Market

Single-family homes, condominiums, and other properties that people want to live in, are—by far—the most commonly traded real estate. We call this kind of market a *thick market,* meaning that there are lots of buyers and sellers coming to the market and conducting their transactions on a day-to-day basis.

So many people want these properties, and that makes life a whole lot easier when trying to sell a property.

In a *thin market,* the opposite is true. Imagine, for instance, you owned a cigarette factory and wanted to sell it. There might only be three buyers in the entire United States who would be willing to pay you for your cigarette factory. Imagine if one was on vacation in the Philippines, one was focusing on improving their own businesses for that year, and the other was too old to care. In this case, you would just have to wait. To sell your factory, you would have to keep on waiting until one of those three people wanted to buy it. It could be many years.

Not so with single-family homes. There are literally millions of buyers. Of course, it is still possible that your property won't sell immediately, even if you've set an appropriate price. Slow periods can occur, during which buyers who want a particular type of house are simply not buying. However, in a thick market, with so many potential buyers, you will still have a good chance of selling in a reasonable amount of time.

Unique Opportunities

Besides the thick market benefits and the bargains available for home mortgages, there are other advantages to being an owner-occupant. It's easier to work with credit unions, for instance, and home equity lines of credit are much easier to pull out of an owner-occupied home.

Lenders know that the owner-occupant buyer is likely to take better care of properties, so they make additional products available only to homeowners. For instance, a homeowner can currently get a Home Depot loan, totally unsecured by anything at only an 8 percent interest rate, and then spend the money on anything at Home Depot.

All these opportunities stack up in favor of the homeowner, and they make it easier in several ways to enter the real estate business. These opportunities can make a large difference. They reduce the difficulty of the process of real estate investment and may allow a burgeoning real estate investor to have some grace on what is likely to be their first project.

The special treatment and advantages of an owner-occupied home can give some room for the new investor to make a few mistakes that on any other deal could potentially kill their entire profitability.

By beginning with an owner-occupied home investment, you can wade into the real estate arena with a little less risk. It can help you get acclimated to this new field and build an understanding of how real estate can be lucrative for you and how it compares to other investment vehicles. You can begin to see what you need to do better, and how to take advantage of opportunities in the market.

When Buying a Home *Doesn't* Make Sense

If you haven't guessed by now, I'm a big fan of homeownership. I want people to invest their time, money, and love into their communities and their environment, and a huge part of that is homeownership. However, I also want it to be a boon to the people who undertake it. Homeownership should make your life easier, not harder.

While there are many advantages to owning your own home, be aware that there are some situations where homeownership doesn't make any sense financially. Make sure yours isn't one of them before you buy.

Here are a few questions to consider:

- Are you currently renting a place at an exceptionally low rent?

- Are home prices exceptionally high where you want to live?

- Do you have terrible credit?

Under any of these conditions, homeownership may not make sense. Every advantage of homeownership I described has a value; you'll have to determine what that is for yourself, considering your personal situation.

If you're getting a smoking deal from your current landlord, you might want to wait to buy. Research the rental rates around you. If you currently pay 60 percent or less of the market rental rate, you're probably better off just saving your extra money.

You should consider where you want to live and whether it would be wise to purchase there. For instance, if you want to live in a highly desirable or high-density urban center, an owner-occupied investment property might not make sense. Real estate prices in these locations tend to rise much faster than rents do; that's because the competition from other people in those places is more intense. I'm not saying you shouldn't choose to live in those places—they're wonderful—however, be aware that you may be paying a luxury premium that cannot be financially justified for most of the homes in that market.

If you have terrible credit, get to work on repairing that credit before you buy. It's easy to do, doesn't take much time, and can have big payoffs. Without good credit, you'd have to borrow from individuals and hard-money lenders, and they're generally much more expensive than the federally insured homeowner mortgages.

If you don't know much about your credit, I recommend logging on to creditkarma.com. For free, they will provide you your credit score from Equifax and TransUnion and tell you what the biggest things affecting it are. Ask for help on biggerpockets.com or another forum if you need help figuring out what to do to raise it.

CHAPTER THREE

The Power of Debt

USING DEBT TO YOUR ADVANTAGE

Real estate has a secret superpower. It is the most lendable asset in the world; it is easier for a borrower to borrow most or all the money for a piece of real estate than it is for any other asset class. This means that one of the most powerful things a real estate investor will need to learn is how to use debt.

Many people are afraid of debt, and think of it as a negative proposition, but it doesn't have to be this way. Debt allows you to pay for most of an asset using money that is not your own. In real estate, not only is it okay, but it is actually *expected* that you do this. In real estate, we call this debt a mortgage. Debt is so common, and it's such a vital part of real estate investing, that many investors make their living just by employing a thorough understanding of how it works.

Banks will preferentially lend against real estate more than against any other asset class, and this makes sense.

If you were a lender looking at collateral against a debt, which would you prefer: lending against personal property, like a gold necklace, or lending against a piece of real estate whose ownership history is recorded in the county records office?

There are a lot of reasons why mortgages are a primary choice, and that's what we'll go over in this chapter. After learning more, I think that you'll see that debt, when used correctly, is a powerful wealth-generating tool and not the frightening money sink that many people think it is.

Price Competitiveness

You may have noticed that real estate prices are much higher than the prices of the typical assets that most people encounter throughout the course of their lives. For your typical renter, the most expensive object they are likely to encounter is a car.

When you buy a car, depending on how you see debt and what your circumstances are, you may pay for it with cash, or you may pay for it with a loan. Either way, it is not likely to be much more expensive than about $24,000. Luxury, specialty, and collectible cars could cost more than a house, but in general, real estate is much more expensive than cars in terms of the contract price for its exchange.

A median single-family home in Portland, Oregon, as of this writing, would cost over $400,000. The reason that the price is typically so high is that people usually pay for it with someone else's money. They look at each piece of real estate—and you should do this, too—as if it were a tiny business that should make them money rather than cost it. When purchasing a business that makes money, you don't need to pay for the whole business yourself as long as you can find a lender who will accept less in regular payments than the business produces.

This strategy will allow you to pay much more for the property; you can pay not only what you've saved so far, but also a fraction of the future proceeds of the property itself. That's a good thing for the real estate investor.

Often, when people look at the sky-high prices of a debt-driven market, they will take themselves out of the bidding for that property. Our competitors, for example, may not want to pay $400,000 for a piece of property; they may only be comfortable paying $250,000 or $300,000. This is why, if you work on projects that have higher price points, you have a less competitive market in which to play. Of course, we also need to be careful that the properties are in fact worth as much as we're paying for them.

Time Leverage

The process of investing in high-value properties involves less competition, as we've just discussed. In addition, these kinds of investments may allow us to better use our time. Even if you've studied real estate for several years, even if you've become a master of your craft, you still only have twenty-four hours in each day, only around eight of which will be productively applied to working on real estate. You need to make sure you are working on the best projects you can during those eight hours.

When you are working on a $2 million project, any decision will not take any longer than it would for a $100,000 project. However, the earning potential on the $2 million project for that same decision is about *twenty times* greater than that of the $100,000 project.

Buying more value is better. It produces more value in the end, and it allows the person with limited time to focus their time on projects that produce more for them and for others. Debt is the single most effective way we can do that. Most people have limited sums of their own capital to spend on projects. Borrowing from a bank or friends to fund projects allows them to afford much bigger and better projects.

Financing Repairs

Suppose you've selected a high-value property that needs some work, and you've purchased it with a mortgage. Wonderful.

What do you do next?

Once you've purchased the property, debt will also be useful for any modifications that need to be made to the property. Say the property needs a new roof and perhaps new sinks, fixtures, and lights. All that can be financed as well.

This part of the real estate business is sometimes referred to as *residential rehabilitation,* or more commonly, *rehabbing or flipping houses.* It is a mature and well-established industry, and it heavily relies on debt. Lenders have grown accustomed to the idea that rehabbers prefer to have their work funded, as much as possible, by other people's money.

Paid-for improvements to property can sometimes be quite costly. In the case of new construction, the improvements could be responsible for most of the cost of the project. If you are an investor of limited financial means, financial assistance for improvements on your properties can be invaluable. If you can put less of your money into projects that are underway, you can afford to take on new projects. Under these circumstances, you are also more likely to be able to take on larger projects, which will allow you to tap into the benefits of high-value property— price competitiveness and time leverage—that we discussed before.

Remember Your Essential Skills

As you can see, debt can be a great tool for a real estate investor. In the next section of the book, we will continue to learn more about its benefits.

Before we go further, however, I want to reiterate for you what a real estate investor's primary contributions to any project are:

- First, there is the opportunity itself. The investor finds and brings the deal to the people who want it.

- Second, there is the planning. The investor designs a plan that will substantially improve the value of the property and communicates the knowledge of how to execute that plan.

That's really it.

Once an investor has done those two things, they could sell the property and the business plan to a contractor and move on. Note that we haven't even mentioned financing here. You don't have to have any money at all to be good at finding and planning for properties. Writing checks is *not* one of the investor's essential skills.

A good investor must have skill in finding good opportunities and making viable plans. These are the hard parts of the process. Investors whose financial means are subject to some restrictions can look for people to do the easy parts for them—like paying for the project.

DOING MORE AND MAKING MORE

How do the benefits of debt show up in actual numbers?

In what other ways is debt useful to a real estate investor?

How can a real estate investor use debt to make more money?

Debt Can Help You Take on More Projects

When a real estate investor's finances are limited, they can release some of the pressure limiting them by taking on debt to do their projects. Accessing this additional money, at reasonable rates, could pay for most of each project for them, allowing the investor to do more projects than they otherwise would be able to.

If this real estate investor uses their skill on a single project, that's wonderful. They will make the profit of a single project. However, you can clearly see that this skill is broadly applicable; the investor could potentially use it again and again.

Like most real estate investors, the limiting factor on how many projects you can take on at once will depend on your available time and the amount of cash you need to reserve control of properties. Using debt can help you relieve some of those limitations, so that you can afford to tackle as many projects as you have time to work on.

You Can Profit More From Your Expertise

We talked about this a little bit in the introduction. A real estate investor who is making money according to their skills and education will make more money by helping more people.

For example, let's say you have skill and knowledge in the area of renovation of single-family homes. The more time you can spend on that particular skill, the better off you will be. If you can hire out the various jobs that need to be done in other areas of the project and be paid only for your expertise, you will be paid more for the number of projects that you can apply your expertise to. Debt allows you to do more of what you want to be good at, which is finding and processing huge deals—and doing more means making more.

Debt Allows You to Keep Money in Your Pocket

One important application of debt is the reduction of out-of-pocket payment for a property. Let's say you have $100,000, and the property costs $100,000. You have two options to purchase it. Either you hand over your $100,000, or you hand over $30,000 and have a bank pay the other $70,000.

Which would you rather do?

Obviously, the option with debt will ultimately cost more money because of the interest on the loan, but before that interest comes due you'd have an extra $70,000 cash and a brand-new income stream that pays for the new debt because that's what you bought it to do.

I would argue that in most cases, having the bank pay the $70,000 and keeping the rest of the money in your own pocket is the safer route. It will also allow you to take advantage of more opportunities later.

We already talked about why a real estate investor might want to take on more opportunities. Let's talk a little bit about why it would be safer.

Suppose the project doesn't go exactly as planned. Let's say a water pipe bursts on the property, and a major repair needs to be done to the plumbing. In addition, all the water-damaged goods will have to be replaced.

I contend that you would be very happy to have kept that $70,000 in your pocket under these circumstances. If you had cash to apply to the unexpected expenses, you could go on with your project without wasting time, and you wouldn't have to explain the situation to any of your third-party investors. Without that cash, the only alternative at this point would be to ask for more funding to pay for the repairs.

Making the Most of Your Limited Resources

To close out this chapter, I would like to introduce the concept of *capital efficiency*. Money works for us, and the capital efficiency of an investment describes how well it is working for us.

Imagine you took $100,000 and put it into a certificate of deposit (CD) at the bank. Current interest rates on CDs are around 1 percent. Imagine you came back a year later. You could expect that CD to have paid out interest payments throughout the year that would have added up to about $1000. Then you still have the CD itself, which is worth $100,000, so at the end of the year, you would have $101,000.

Now, imagine instead that your CD paid 10 percent per year. At the end of the year, you would have $110,000, although you started with that same $100,000. The $110,000 CD we would say was *more capital efficient*. That means you get more bang for your buck. You put down the same money, but you get more cash out of the deal at the end of the year.

The same can be said about real estate projects. If you have $100,000 and are trying to make it go as far as you can, chances are good that you'll need to use debt to do that. When the project itself has higher returns than the debt, that debt, when properly negotiated, can dramatically improve your capital efficiency. When an investor can amplify their percentage returns using debt, we call that *leverage*.

GETTING OFF THE TARGET

It's helpful to take a new mindset toward money when dealing with large quantities of debt. The specific amount the debt is worth is a lot less important than the positioning that it has relative to the real estate it's associated with and the income that real estate creates. This is because debt has a little-known asset-protection function that makes a real estate investor less attractive to the lawyers that wander our fair country.

A Litigious Environment

There is a joke that a small town that cannot support one lawyer can always support two. There is a substantial component of the American economy that is devoted to the legal dispute of anything and everything. I hesitate to call it justice because it's often not at all about justice.

In real estate transactions, having debt can provide a protective advantage in this litigious environment. Large piles of cash or large piles of equity, such as exist in properties that don't have any debt against them, can be sold to produce a nice, attractive payout for someone who doesn't want to be involved in the property for the long term. A lawyer can sue to force the sale of a property, and this is more likely to happen when there is easy financial gain for their client.

In this case, debt can be helpful because whenever debt occupies most of the value of the property, it reduces the benefit to someone who can force the sale of the property; the lender can and should rightly declare that if the property is sold, most of its proceeds should go back to the lender.

Small Equity Portions

When a lender lends against a property, they'll typically ask for what is called a *trust deed*. That trust deed makes the lender the legal owner of the property, managed by a trustee. A trust deed is required to be reconveyed, or eliminated, upon any liquidity event, say a sale or refinance, to ensure that the lender is treated fairly.

If there is a lawsuit that affects a property and the property is sold to satisfy the judgments of the lawsuit, the lender, no matter what the lawsuit was about, is probably going to be entirely innocent of any sort of wrongdoing associated in the lawsuit. They would rightly deserve their money back.

If most of the value of a property is owed to a lender, say 70 percent, then that means that even if the forced sale sold the property for 100 percent of its value, only 30 percent would be left over. However, forced sales are not ideal sales. They may sell for only 75 to 80 percent, leaving only small sums left over for the lawyer and his client who forced the sale.

You can see how debt can protect the real estate investor by making them less of a target for forced sales. If a lawyer can see that proceeds from any forced sale would be minimal, they are less likely to pursue a case that may cost them a large amount of time and turn up very little in the end.

Profit Through Cash Flow

The next question you may naturally ask is: *Jeff, if I can't ever own my real estate, how will I ever make money? Won't I always be handing it over to my lenders?*

That is probably true for most of the money that you make. If you buy a $400,000 asset and pay for $300,000 of it by borrowing from a friend, they would rightfully deserve a substantial chunk of the profits.

However, if you are a disciplined real estate deal underwriter, you will make sure there is always some cash left over from the profits of the operation of the property. That is profit. That will be yours. It will also be *residual,* meaning it will be treated as a passive income source, which will be advantageously taxed by the federal government. It will continue coming in as you move on to bigger and better things.

Further, as the property increases in value or as it pays down the debt, you will occasionally have opportunities to get another loan against the property you already own. That loan, if it is underwritten so that it can still be paid for by the property, will behave like profit to the investor. As a result, you'll be able to take that money out and spend it on whatever you like, even though it must be repaid to the lender.

What all this means is that instead of owning a free and clear property, which itself has little value, you will claim your pay in monthly cash flow of the property over time and a large cash payment every five years or so in the form of a refinance or new loan.

CHAPTER FOUR

The Wind at Our Backs

POLITICS

Politics has an impact on all businesses, including real estate, and it is helpful to understand the nature of this impact. This section will give you some useful information.

There isn't much that a politician would consider more important than jobs and the economy. Politicians always like to talk about what they are going to do to create new jobs, or how they're going to bring more jobs home from other countries.

So, how does real estate figure into this topic?

Well, real estate is one of the core concepts behind American business, and it is one of the biggest job creators in the country. A large portion of our economy is devoted directly to real estate and to jobs related to real estate. Fortunately, the people who make our laws and manage our government understand this. For real estate investors, some helpful elements have been incorporated into the political structure. Society helps investors significantly in many ways, and we will discuss them in this chapter.

Grants

Grant programs are designed to give people money for projects that support an objective. One way that society helps real estate investors do more of what they do is by offering grants. Many programs give people money to invest in real estate. The largest and most traded real estate market type—and best funded by government grants—is housing.

Many people in our population have problems accessing housing. It is fairly common that people of lesser means cannot pay enough in rent to entice entrepreneurs to go through the trouble of producing housing to sell to them. There are political programs designed to help people with these problems, and, as part of these programs, grants are given to real estate investors who are willing to do the job.

These grant programs are meant to give money away to people who add value in a particular way, within the real estate market. If your project idea, if your plan, if your scheme to add value is something that you think might be interesting to a grant program, take some time to check them out.

Find out if there are any grants for the type of work that you want to do. At the website *grants.gov,* you can find more information, including which agencies offer grants, what the requirements are, and how to navigate through the grant application process.

Society Wants Us to Do What We're Doing

Even if your business plan turns out to be mostly for-profit and is uninteresting to grant writers, if it is designed to add value, chances are that our society still wants you to execute it because it's likely to make all of us wealthier if it succeeds.

For example, suppose you construct a bed-and-breakfast (B&B). That B&B will create a comfortable place for visitors to stay when they come to your town or city. The visitors are happy to pay; they'd rather have a place to stay than keep the cash they pay you. A B&B will also need people to service it, so it helps creates jobs. The workers are happy because they have steady employment that allows them to buy the things they want, and they can count on you to protect them from the variabilities of the market. You're happy because you get paid.

Everybody wants your B&B to exist, and because of this, the laws, for the most part, make it reasonably easy to proceed with these kinds of projects.

Getting People to See the Value

If you have a value proposition and it really does improve society in some way, the biggest problem you're likely to run into is a lack of understanding. If the people you present it to don't understand it or don't trust certain aspects of it, it will be difficult to move forward. While presenting your idea, you must communicate the value and the plan clearly to ensure its acceptance.

Keep in mind that people are afraid of what they don't understand. Put thought into your communication strategy. Your target audience will not be able to appreciate your value proposition if they don't understand it.

THE INTERNAL REVENUE SERVICE

The IRS runs our country's tax structure, as you know. What you might not know is that the tax system is one of the most common means by which the government attempts to encourage or discourage certain behaviors. The government taxes activities they don't like at a higher rate, while behaviors they want to encourage are taxed less. The IRS offers incentives to industries that the government wants to encourage. Tax advantages are some of the most common incentives. Tax advantages can sometimes even be sold to people with more use for them.

Depreciation

One of the main ways that the IRS encourages real estate development and investment is through depreciation. Since prices for real estate are often substantial compared to their cash flow, this can be particularly helpful. Depreciation allows real estate investors to take an expensive asset and break the price of it up into yearly losses that make their investment, for tax purposes, appear to be unprofitable. This is to account for the loss in value of the property, or *depreciation*. However, in real estate, the real loss in value of the property over the years and as you use it can be quite small. In fact, the value of real estate usually goes up with the passage of time.

To give you an idea, the IRS currently allows depreciation of residential property over twenty-seven-and-a-half years. That is to say, one pretends the residential property, such as a house, has a usable life of twenty-seven-and-a-half years, and after this time, the house would be used up, done with, expended. However, most people understand that a house could last for one hundred years or more. That imaginary loss in twenty-seven-and-a-half years can make a real estate project more tax-efficient by creating the appearance of less profit upfront and thus make it less of a tax burden. Tax-wise, this is a big advantage for the real estate industry; other industries are treated not so kindly.

Itemized Deductions

The other way the IRS assists real estate investors—and it does this for most businesses—is in business expense deductions. All the expenditures involved in executing your business plan, say in the rental of a single-family home, can be deducted as business expenses. This includes a wide variety of items, like the inspection of the property on a regular basis, or the care of the lawn.

Many costs that you incur while conducting your business can be deducted as business expenses. Taking care to record and document the expenses that you have anyway but are ultimately for business purposes can help you save some money.

Are you eating dinner with some people whom you like?

Could they be potential clients?

If the answer is yes, talk some business with them and then write the dinner off as a *meals and entertainment* expense.

Do you want to visit Hawaii?

Is there any business you could do in Hawaii?

Go visit, do the business, and write the trip off your taxes.

Filing Structure

Another way the IRS helps real estate investors is by their differentiation from other types of entities. We're allowed to report our income in a couple different ways with the IRS. Before I say more though, know this: if you're going to be in business, you need a Certified Public Accountant (CPA).

I recommend you study the tax law yourself to some extent so that you can be sure you and your CPA are on the same page, but you need to be spending most of your time creating business plans and driving revenue. Unless you are a CPA, it won't be worth the time you would spend studying the law to determine how best to do your taxes.

That said, you will find that corporations, sole proprietorships, partnerships, and real estate investment trusts (REITs) are all taxed differently and often in ways that can be used to your advantage. Your CPA can help you find the most advantageous filing structure for your business.

THE FEDERAL RESERVE

One of the strongest winds at our back is the Federal Reserve. They control the money supply, and for a business, this has an effect that is particularly beneficial to real estate investors. I'll tell you why in this chapter.

The Money Supply

You probably don't think about it very much, but money is actually a thing traded just like anything else. It has its own value, and that value can change. If you were to take lawn chairs, for instance, and decided to buy and sell lawn chairs, you would realize that lawn chairs change in value from one year to the next, from one season to the next, and from location to location.

It's the same with money. Money is more or less valuable depending on where it is, what time it is, and what date it is. The value of money is constantly changing, and sometimes it is intentionally manipulated.

A person selling lawn chairs could create a false scarcity of a particular type of lawn chair in an attempt to drive up the price. The same can happen with money. The Federal Open Market Committee—the committee that runs the Federal Reserve—will attempt to change the value of money and often does, usually to decrease the value of the money. I will tell you more about that in the inflation section of this chapter, but for now, keep in mind that inflation is a decrease in the value of a currency, and the Federal Reserve works to make sure it happens.

Interest and Fixed-Price Contracts

Before we do talk about inflation, I'd like to talk about another thing that people often do regarding money. The most common way to construct financial instruments is in the form of debt or loans. People lend someone money, and then expect to receive it back with interest. That is fine, and that can be a profitable undertaking for the lender.

However, most debt is constructed in the form of a fixed payback; that is to say, if you borrow one hundred dollars, you should pay back one hundred dollars, plus the interest, which let's say is 10 percent. You would pay back one hundred dollars of principal, plus ten dollars, which is 10 percent of the hundred-dollar principal, or one hundred and ten dollars.

That sounds fine, but to understand this process fully, you must keep in mind that the intent of the loan is to change the location of money *in time*. If the value of money changes over time, that impacts the investment.

For example, if a loan is over the course of a year, a borrower might take out one hundred dollars at the beginning of the year and pay it back at the end of the year. As we just discussed, money changes value depending on what date it is. If a borrower takes out a loan on January 1 of some year, and then pays it back on December 31 of that same year, the money that they are paying back may very well be of a totally different value. This is a huge deal. You must understand this to understand the power of any business that creates real value using money.

Inflation

If a debt is created by borrowing a fixed sum of dollars and returning another fixed sum of dollars, we call that fixed-price debt. Fixed-price debt is affected by inflation. As I told you earlier, the Federal Reserve attempts to reduce the value of money. Currently, their target is around 2 percent per year. That has a substantial effect on real estate investors because they tend to borrow most of their money on fixed-price contracts. They use that money to buy real assets that they expect to either not change in value or to go up.

For the moment, let's assume they don't change in value. The real estate investor uses that piece of real estate that has not changed in value to pay back the money that has lost value.

Let me restate that, just in case it wasn't clear.

A real estate investor borrows $100,000 to buy an asset. The asset pays for the loan, then, over time, even though the investor has done nothing of his or her own accord, they owe less value than they did before. This means he could either restructure his operations to make more money or sell the asset for more than what was paid. That is huge.

To put it another way, imagine if, instead of borrowing one hundred dollars and paying back one hundred ten, you could borrow one hundred dollars and pay back ninety-eight.

Wouldn't that be a significant advantage?

Inflation is exactly that. A person in an inflationary environment pays back less value per dollar than they borrow simply because they borrowed the money in the past and they will pay it back in the future. In the past, the money was worth more, but in the future, it will be worth less. It is likely that the longer the borrower holds the loan, the longer they'll benefit from this sort of phenomenon.

What does this look like with respect to the prices on the market?

It looks like the asset *rises in value*. The asset may indeed be rising in value, but often what's happening is the money is losing value. Inflation is stealthy.

The interesting thing about inflation and the changing value of money is that it's not an accident. The Federal Reserve targets a specific inflation rate. They don't have the last word on the value of money, but they certainly have an influence. For the most part, they tend to get what they want. What they want is for the value of money to decline.

Real estate investors can build their whole business just around that concept. I wouldn't recommend depending on it alone, but it is a valuable portion of the way that real estate investors make a profit.

CHAPTER FIVE

Bigger Is Better –
In Real Estate, Size Does Matter

The primary advantage of real estate is the ability to make investments predominantly, or even entirely, with other people's money. The second advantage is one that people often see as a disadvantage, and that is the projects are bigger than other investments.

Real estate simply costs more than almost any other type of asset that can be purchased.

If you consider shares of a publicly traded company, such as Boeing, for instance, they can usually be acquired on the order of one hundred dollars per share.

In real estate, you'd be hard pressed to find any piece of real property selling for less than $1000. In desirable locations, real estate sells for multiple hundreds of thousands. While this may seem like a disadvantage, to an educated and savvy investor, this is one of the biggest advantages of real estate. Here is why.

SIZE MATTERS TO YOU

You Can Only Work on so Many Projects

The first reason that size is an advantage is scalability with respect to time. You only have so many hours in a day, only so many days in a week, only so many weeks in a year.

In an extreme case, suppose that you were selling pencils for a nickel each, and you made one cent of commission on each one. That is 20 percent commission, which is a good commission. You also have a friend who runs a reliable business and who would hire you for minimum wage to do paperwork. For you to make as much money selling pencils as minimum wage—let's say fourteen dollars per hour—you'd have to sell one thousand four hundred pencils per hour.

That'd be millions of pencils per year just to make minimum wage.

In real estate, on the other hand, if you were to collect a standard commission on a $500,000 trade of real property, you'd only have to sell two properties. You could sell millions of pencils per year, but you'd better not do it one at a time. If all you had to do to sell a pencil was shake someone's hand, you still wouldn't be able to keep up. However, you could sell one at a time in real estate if each piece sells at $500,000, and you would have the time to cultivate relationships with your buyers and your sellers and to make sure that you managed the process right for each one.

You Can Only Hold So Many Professions

Furthermore, after you get involved in real estate, you will realize that there are many different aspects of it. There are many ways to add value to your investment. Properties can be framed, finished, or improved. There is house-wrapping work. There is legal work. There is accounting work. Some people try to do it all. From an infinite time perspective, that would be fine, and they would have extremely profitable projects because they are providing their value in so many ways.

However, as we've discussed before, we run out of time; there are only so many hours in the day. If a project has one thousand hours of work to be done on it, and you do it all yourself, you would be limited to two projects per year.

Now, I don't recommend that you do all your own work. I know I'm not qualified for everything that happens in my projects, and you probably aren't either. The point is that I *could* be. I won't because on larger projects, it is more convenient and more financially sensible to hire other people to do some of the work. Then I can use my real- estate expertise to take on more projects.

I'll go into more detail about how larger projects help make it easier to hire other people later in this chapter.

You Must Leverage Your Time

As far as your time is concerned, you want to maximize the value you're creating. Let's use money to measure value, despite its imperfections. Value creation is usually measured as a percentage of value put in. If a project costs $100,000, and it sells for $110,000, we say that the return was 10 percent.

How would this change for a million-dollar project?

You could still expect to make 10 percent, which on a million-dollar project is $100,000, but the amount of work to be done is not amplified nearly as much. A million-dollar project does not take ten times as much work as a $100,000 project.

Let's suppose it takes twice as much work. If you make ten times as much money for only twice as much work, you're being much more efficient with your time on larger projects.

The most valuable thing that any person possesses is their time. I can't emphasize this enough. If you are going to spend your time making money, as opposed to doing something that might be more personally fulfilling, you will want to do it as efficiently as possible. I recommend that you find some niche in real estate that allows you to enjoy it as well, but whatever you do, do it in a manner that is efficient according to what you want to get out of it. For real estate, that generally means bigger projects. Do more. Leverage your time to accomplish as much as possible.

SIZE MATTERS TO YOUR CLIENTS

In the previous chapter, I mentioned that it's easier to pay people for the various trades involved with a real estate project on a larger project than it is on a smaller project. In this chapter, I will describe why that is and how it helps everyone involved.

Better Pay for You

As I discussed in the previous chapter, it's easier to be paid better on larger projects. This goes across the board. If you're getting paid 10 percent of the project, then you can get paid better for what is usually only slightly more work.

Let's compare the $100,000 project and the million-dollar project that we looked at before. If you're getting 10 percent, that's $10,000 on the $100,000 project and $100,000 on the million-dollar project. Let's say you're doing twice as much work on the million-dollar project. In this case, your pay equivalent per hour is still five times that of the smaller project.

Bigger projects have a degree of generosity that is not available for smaller, tighter projects. You can be more generous with your own time as well, so you can do a better job, paying more attention to the details on those projects. You can also be more generous with the various other people with whom you work on the project.

Better Pay for Them

Let's say that you're hiring a realtor on a $100,000 project. A realtor's standard commission fee on a project would be 3 percent on a sale. On a $100,000 project, that is $3,000. On a million-dollar project, that would be $30,000.

Supposing that the realtor only had to do twice as much work for the million-dollar project as for the $100,000 project, they would effectively be getting $15,000 for the same work that they earned $3,000 for on the smaller project.

Let's suppose you wanted to cut a deal. Three percent might be too high on the million-dollar project. If you cut that in half, the realtor would still be making five times as much as they would on a $100,000 project. That's great. They will appreciate the better compensation of their efforts, even after you've negotiated down the total price. You'll pay less of the percentage of the project, and they'll still make more.

Better Service

Imagine for the moment that you're that realtor getting paid five times as much for working with one client as opposed to working with another client.

If that were the case, do you think that you would tend to do a little extra for that?

For example, perhaps you would take the time to sit down and write up an offering memorandum, or to create some marketing materials that you might not otherwise for a more run-of-the-mill deal.

That's exactly what you can expect on larger real estate projects. In fact, often the best practitioners—like the best contractors, for instance—will not work on smaller projects because they simply don't pay well enough for the quality of work that the contractors want to do. The same goes with realtors and for most of the trades inside the real estate industry.

If your service providers do a better job handling challenges that come up, you will run into fewer obstacles that are simply the result of the chaotic world that we live in. When you're getting higher quality work from the people you hire, it is easier to make those projects successful.

SIZE MATTERS TO YOUR COMPETITORS

Another reason that size matters so much in real estate is perhaps the most obvious: competition. We work in competitive marketplaces, and whenever we can avoid situations where we are competing with many other players, we can allow ourselves more freedom and more flexibility in what can be done. The entire process becomes less stressful as well.

The Fear of Real Estate

There is probably no more common thought that keeps people out of investing in real estate than the one that follows: *Oh, that is too expensive for me.*

Picture a person who encounters a piece of real estate that costs more than any sane person would ever keep on hand. They will likely remove themselves from the game. When looking at a property that costs $500,000, even a 20 percent down payment on that property will be more than anything that most people will buy in a typical day, week, or even year. Most people will decide it's too much and will take themselves out of the competition. That is advantageous to the people who remain *in* because then they need to contend with fewer players.

Being Priced Out of the Market

That reaction to high-priced real estate is totally reasonable, but it kind of misses the point. Real estate is about value, not about price.

Think of it this way: *If I'm getting $600,000 worth of value, then it is totally reasonable to pay $500,000 worth of price.*

Suppose you were buying gold. If someone told you the gold they had for sale would cost $500,000, you would ask how much gold they had. Then you would go to a gold exchange, look up the current price of gold, and compare what they were asking to the current market value of the gold they were selling.

That's exactly the way real estate works. Two people make their own assessment, and when they disagree, there is an opportunity.

The fear remains because many people don't trust their ability to assess the value of a piece of real estate. In addition, most people don't understand the methods that are necessary to pay for a piece of real estate that is higher priced than they can pay out of their own pocket. They don't understand how to syndicate. They are afraid to borrow money. They haven't formed the proper connections with other people who can afford them the opportunities to pay for those larger pieces of real estate.

That fear is what can create an opportunity for you, if you are knowledgeable, have connections, and are unafraid to borrow money to purchase a piece of real estate that most people would be terrified to purchase themselves.

Bringing Your Friends with You

How do you keep from being priced out of the market?

The first and simplest way is to get over your fear of debt. Borrowing money is the most common and cheapest way to pay for real estate.

There are two keys to borrowing money. The first is that every time you do so, you match it with a plan that pays for the debt, interest, and principal. Every business plan can pay for a certain amount of debt, but you can't create any more debt than that business plan can pay for, or that all your total business plans can pay for.

The second key is to bring your friends with you. For everything in excess of that debt, you will probably use equity provided by capital partners who will take on the risk of the deal to support your business plan and to make the project happen. So, make friends. Talk to people. Find out who else is interested in real estate.

Who else is interested in the type of project you want to work on?

Who wants to support you?

When you have found people who are willing and able to help you make the project happen, take note. Put them on a list of people to contact whenever you have an opportunity. Make sure you maintain those relationships so that when you're ready to go, they are too.

Conclusion

I hope I've made it clear to you through the course of this book that real estate can be a powerful tool for generating wealth. The generation of profit is the part of a real estate project that makes it sustainable, that makes a person able to go on and do more in a capitalistic society that expects people to be profitable at their work. However, it's only one facet of being a real estate entrepreneur.

What I really want is for people to get paid well for making the world a better place. Everything eventually ties back to that. If you have an idea how to make the world better, then I also want you to know how to make it profitable so that you can be well rewarded for executing your plans.

If you are currently a renter, and you've finished this book, I hope you see that buying a home can be an advantageous financial proposition. If you haven't begun any real estate projects yet, I recommend that one be your first. There is so much grease for the wheels on the owner-occupant proposition, and that makes success more likely.

Assess whether buying a home really is something you are interested in doing. Start thinking about what you might want to buy, and where. Talk to real estate agents about the market conditions in the places you want to live so you can learn what to expect when buying a home in your area. When you are ready, start looking at properties.

If you already own a home and you are a bit more familiar with the process, then start thinking about real estate investments that would challenge you. There are many options, depending on your experience level. You could consider adding an extension to your home, or buying a rental property, or maybe partitioning off a piece of the land and building another home there.

Finally, whatever you do, make sure you have fun with it! There's too much opportunity out there in the world not to.

Next Steps

By now, I hope you're feeling a little bit excited about the prospects that real estate has for you. Scan some Zillow listings and talk to some real estate agents to get an idea of what's available. If this is your first encounter with real estate, check out a few more sources to learn more about the process before you buy.

An excellent website for continuing education in real estate is *biggerpockets.com*.

If you're interested in my work, you can follow my company's activity at *dynamicrealestateinnovations.com* and read about some of the properties we're currently working on.

You can also follow the company through our Facebook page, *Dynamic Real Estate Innovations*, where you'll learn about our live events and other opportunities that may come up.

About the Author

Jeffrey Stump is a real estate investor, capital raiser, and speaker. He spends most of his time arranging new-construction apartment real estate deals in the Portland, Oregon, area and educating people about the ways that urban life can contribute to health, wealth, and happiness. He and his business partner, Jose, own and operate a real estate investment company that they use to make urban infill improvements to the built environment.

Jeffrey attended The University of Texas at Austin and received a bachelor's degree in civil engineering and a master's degree focusing on structural engineering.

Before, during, and after school, he worked in single-family home construction, engineering education, and bridge inspection. Realizing he had the capacity to do much more, in 2015, he and Jose co-founded Dynamic Real Estate Innovations, LLC (DREI), and began finding and executing real estate deals in the Portland area.

Jeffrey is a graduate of the *Train the Trainer* program from Success Resources America, and currently provides training designed to excite people and educate them about the core principles of real estate investment.

He trains about real estate because he believes that environment is stronger than willpower for better or worse, but especially for better.

Jeffrey believes that we can use the tools available in real estate investing to create built environments that naturally incline the people living in them to adopt behaviors that make them healthier, wealthier, and happier. He therefore seeks out people who are motivated to help him create spaces like that or who are motivated to create those spaces themselves. He works to help people understand how to do this kind of work and be well rewarded for it.

23116050R00062

Made in the USA
San Bernardino, CA
23 January 2019